Touching the Body
Reaching the Soul

Touching the Body
Reaching the Soul

How Touch Influences
the Nature of Human Beings

by

Sandra Dillon Wooten

TAOS
MOUNTAIN
PRESS

Published in the United States of America by
Taos Mountain Press
223 N. Guadalupe #288
Santa Fe, New Mexico 87501
Phone: 505-820-2882   Fax: 505-820-2883
e-mail: TaosMtn@aol.com

For information on classes, contact
Rosen Method Center Southwest
P.O. Box 344, Santa Fe, New Mexico 87504
Phone: (505) 982-7149   e-mail: sw.touch@ix.netcom.com
http://www.mcn.org/b/rosen/swrc.html

Book design by Sharyn Venit
Photograph on page 41 by Cameron Hough
Copy editing by Judy Johnstone
Printed by Cloud Bridge Printers, Santa Fe, New Mexico

First published in October 1995
Second printing, January 1997

ISBN 0-9654790-0-5

10 9 8 7 6 5 4 3

Acknowledgements

To my husband Jerry, whose love and constant support has touched me more than words can say, I offer my deepest gratitude and pray we will be touching each other for another thirty-five years...at least. To John whose words, "Go for it, Mom !" kept ringing in my heart as I wrote; and who, through marriage, has given us Suzanne, Michele, Hailey, and Jasmine, a great blessing, indeed; I love and admire you. To Laurie, whose touch I experience, but cannot explain, my eternal love.

I have had a wonderful group of people encourage and guide me in the writing of this book and I am very grateful. To David Schwartz, without whom this book would never have been written, I thank you for your "nudging", commitment, kind words and patience. I am indebted and grateful to Lois Silverstein, excellent editor, and friend, whose eagle eye, expertise, and kind heart showed me the way. A special thank you to Eric Greenleaf, mentor and friend, whose guidance and kindness has meant so much, and who, along with Deborah Joy, Linda Silver and Pat Murphy, formed our 'Reflecting Team' consultation group that is unsurpassed in professional knowledge, skill and respect. Thank you all for your help, wit and humor! To Sharyn Venit, Taos Mountain Press, your belief in this book, your creativity, and your invaluable help is appreciated more than I can say. To Marion Rosen, teacher and mentor, and to my students and clients, from whom I have learned so much, thank you, all.

About This Book...

This book is an important contribution to the growing body of knowledge about the intricate relationship between psychological issues and the physical body. These issues are of direct relevance to the work of hospital and home care nurses, doctors, psychotherapists, massage therapists, physical therapists, bodyworkers, hospice workers, clergy and other health care providers. Experiences cited as examples in this book are drawn from the author's years of work as a Rosen Method practitioner.

To quote the author: *"Respectful touch allows changes to begin on the inside, and move outward at a pace that matches an individual's own rhythm. The result is an 'unfolding.' Rather than attempting to fix someone or make them different, this is a process of gently showing people to themselves— reflecting their true being, recognizing their integrity & aliveness, allowing physical ease."*

Table of Contents

Introduction

Touch is one of the most profound and influential experiences a human being can have, yet, little attention has been given to, or research done on, the impact of touch on human beings.

The type of touch we experience as infants forms, informs and defines us. As adults, touch continues to influence our physical, emotional, attitudinal and spiritual nature. Touch not only influences how we move and react and/or respond to our environment, but, how we know and experience ourselves.

Here I write about human touch and inquire about the interface and relationship between touch and consciousness, touch and physics, and touch and creative expression in order to clarify the profound influence touch has on each one of us. During my research these different relationships touched and flowed into each other, unfolding in the way a Rosen Method bodywork session unfolds for a client: I inquired into the relationship of touch and consciousness and this became a field of exploration and discovery. Then, the next layer emerged, and my inquiry flowed from one awareness and study into another, moving forward and deepening. The body of this book is a work in process.

Personal History

"Define the word 'touch' for me", a longtime friend asked. "I want to know more."

My mind went blank at her request. At that moment, nothing came to mind. A few words would begin to form and then dart away, unknown and impossible to catch. Her question began my search to define this word touch I could not grasp. The more I thought about touch, the more it seemed undefinable; I could, however, find many words that spoke to my *experience* of touch: calming, reassuring, relaxing, generous, loving, heartfelt, stimulating, warm. I also knew touch to be painful, shocking, anger-provoking, stunning. I remembered from my own childhood that lack of touch could stimulate painful experiences. The longer I thought about the word touch, many more words came: rejection, loss, hurt, anger, and loneliness. As a child I realized I could not really know my inner self or even where I began or ended physically, without the experience of being touched and touching others. Contemplating little or no touch at all, I felt fearful and even questioned my own existence ! I knew my experience of being touched and touching others was essential to my survival.

My earliest memory is of lying on a large bed with my mother beside me. To this day I can recall her hand, gentle upon my back, calming me for my afternoon nap. I must have been around two years old at the time. Later, I remember sitting next to her while she read to me and absentmindedly stroked my arm. I cuddled up next to her, molding my body to hers, not wanting to miss a word, or her touch. Throughout those early years I did not have to think about her touching me, she was simply within easy reach; whenever I wanted or needed contact.

The day before my sixth birthday I was taken by my father to stay with my grandmother for a few days. Grandma had a family birthday party for me and I remember I was puzzled because it was a happy occasion and yet, I felt unhappy. I felt lonely. I had never been away from my mother before. I spent the night in Grandma's small back bedroom and awoke hearing the mourning doves. The air was rent with sadness. I had never experienced such a feeling. Today I could describe it as a felt sense of loss, but then, I just didn't know what to do or where to turn. Nor, for the most part, did I know what was expected of me since Grandma had her own routine around the house and she kept busy. One memory of being included in her routine stands out clearly amid the feelings of loss, that was making bread with her. I was so happy to be a part of this work that, for a while, I forgot my loneliness.

My task was to form small balls of dough for cloverleaf rolls. She taught me by *standing close* to me and showing me how to use my hands. I learned three things: it was very important not to work the dough too much; that three balls of dough needed to be placed gently but firmly in the cupcake pan for each cloverleaf roll; and, that with *her hands on mine* I learned easily and quickly to know when the texture and shape of the dough was correct. The task ended far too quickly for me, and I was again aware of my sadness. My grandmother never asked how I felt. In fact, no one seemed to notice me at all except in the usual ways; that is, about my getting dressed and eating meals and asking how school was today; I had just started first grade. I told no one how I felt for I didn't know how; I had never heard anyone talk about feelings. I did know I was at grandma's because my mother went to the hospital to get a new baby. I had been excited about THAT, but I surely , at that time, did not expect nor did I know the wrenching cost this change in my life would have on me and my well-being. Days later when I returned home, there was my new brother.

I do not recall my mother ever touching me again in her warm and loving manner.

I have very few memories of other events in my early childhood but from the time my brother was born I can say how I felt. Empty. My mother no longer rubbed my back, sat me next to her to read a story or touched me in any way whatsoever that invited me into her warmth. I felt the lack of her touch in a deeply physical way and would sometimes ask her to rub my arm. She would then, but in a perfunctory way, leaving me after feeling as helpless and lonely as I had before I found the courage to ask her. I soon stopped asking.

I'm searching deeply inside of myself to access these memories, for it took a very short time for me to put away the distress I felt then. I know now I learned to keep my emotions to myself and not ask for what I wanted and needed by physically contracting. I learned to have no expectations that anyone in my family was interested in how I felt or who I was. I loved my brother and was excited about school. My life took on the cast of a happy childhood; I loved going to school, riding my bike, climbing trees, playing jacks and being with neighborhood friends. My mother was busy with my brother as well as cleaning house and Women's Fellowship at the church. She cooked meals and mended my clothes and shopped. She spent hours sewing labels in my sister's clothing because Deanne went away to the School for the Deaf during the school year. I did not know I was emotionally neglected or that my mother was critical and cold to me until much later, when I had a family of my own. I was just living my life. We appeared to be a happy family with grandparents, aunts, uncles and cousins gathering frequently. I did not know something essential was missing for me: my mother's touch.

My mother died when I was 29 years old. My family and I were living in California but I flew home to spend several weeks with her while she was in the hospital. I spent days sitting with her, and toward the end of her life, sat holding her hand for hours on end. Often her hand would move gently over mine and evoke my early experience of her touch.

The bonding we had made in this life was through the touching. Without it there was no real connection between us. The loss of her touch in my life was crucial to my development. In grade school and as a teenager, this loss influenced how I chose friends; I often reached out to people who were not warm and outgoing, but critical of others and distant in their expression of emotions. My playmates often teased me and were critical, and I would feel unwanted. Lack of touch had a huge impact on my inability to relax and play, listen to myself and know what I was feeling. In essence, it was as if there was one piece missing in a huge jigsaw puzzle; without that piece, no matter how well put together the puzzle was, it simply was not a coherent whole. Life seemed solemn to me. People who were warm, loving and accepting of me were the exception in my life, and I cherished the ones I had.

When I was nineteen years old I met a woman who would change my life. I met her through a friend and colleague of my husband's on an unforgettably clear and sunny October day in Berkeley. Meeting her then was the beginning of the role she played in my destiny. It was a brief meeting; we were only at Marion's home to introduce her to some friends of ours who wanted to consult with her. Even so, to this day I remember how aware I was as we drove up to her house, and how I felt as I slowly walked up her uneven steps, gazing with wonder at the flowers in her garden. I felt anticipation and curiosity, as if an adventure were about to begin. When she opened her kitchen door, greeted us with a shy smile and invited us in, I was struck by the stark simplicity of her home. There were flowers on her kitchen table, but no curtains at the windows. The living room was furnished with a piano and sofa, and a table, which was at one end of the long, narrow room. The room, while nearly empty, certainly did not feel that way to me; rather, I sensed comfort and simplicity. Then, seven months pregnant and hopeful for my new family, I felt exhilarated and yet calm, and I can still feel my husband's hand in mine as we gazed out her window at San Francisco Bay and the Golden Gate bridge. Her meeting with our friends lasted no more than half an hour and even though I was aware of not really wanting to leave so soon, we were quickly absorbed into the busy city and our own lives.

Eighteen years later, in 1978, I began asking friends if they knew of a therapist who did gentle work on the body. I had some lower back pain off and on and while I had had chiropractic and biofeedback as well as many Polarity Therapy sessions, I was looking for another way to enhance my healing process. I had been inquisitive for many years about healing modalities, had read volumes of books on various healing practices, and now was living near Berkeley where many of the techniques I had read about were available. Still, nothing I came across caught my attention.

I was visiting with a friend one day when she said, "Why don't you go see Marion Rosen? She's a physical therapist who has developed her own kind of work and I hear she's really good ! I don't think its easy to get an appointment, but why not try?" I did. A few days later my back went out, and I was in excruciating pain. I didn't give a second thought as to who to call for help. I called Marion Rosen immediately but in her lilting German accent she quietly informed me she had no available appointments and referred me to someone else. It was several weeks before I called again, but this time she had an opening a few days later. Her office was on Grand Avenue in Oakland in an imposing old building that looked more like a mansion than a site for medical offices. Her office was in the basement. Her patients could either take the rickety elevator down one floor or walk down the curving narrow stairs to end up in a tiny confined hallway she used as a waiting room. While it was hardly inviting, the minute she asked me into her room, I felt comfortable. I did not know what to expect, but somehow I knew I could trust her.

I still clearly remember my first session with Marion Rosen. As I lay on her table and her hand lay gentle and comfortable on my back, the memory of seeing my mother standing in the doorway of my childhood home came to me . It was now seven years since she had died. Suddenly I missed her terribly; I felt an ache in my heart and tears in my eyes. Marion could feel and see my breath change and the muscles in my upper back relax. She asked, "What happened?" I felt very sad as I told her of the memory. Within a few moments, I was aware of her hand on my back again and of an unexpected sense of serenity. Later that evening, while reviewing the session, I was astonished by how the memory, the experience of my sadness and the ensuing physical and emotional relaxation correlated. Excitedly I told my husband about my experience. He was quiet for a moment, intent in his thoughts, then said in a voice filled with remembering, "Marion Rosen. Isn't that Raoul's friend?" Suddenly years were left behind me and I was again standing at her kitchen door looking into her blue eyes.

Two weeks later, as I entered her office for my second appointment, I asked if she could possibly have any memory of meeting me before. With a twinkle in her eye, one I was to see frequently for many years to come from that moment on, she said, "Oh yes, of course I do. The minute I saw the name on your check, I knew." She had not caught my last name when I made the first appointment. She continued to say that she had kept track of us. She had followed my husband's career through her friend who worked with my husband, the same one who had introduced us to Marion eighteen years earlier, and always knew in what part of the country we were living. I was astonished and never thought to ask her why. Perhaps it was because my husband's name would come up in conversation.

By the end of the second session I received from Marion, there was no question in my mind that I wanted to learn the work she was doing. I had not only felt her touch on my body, but felt deeply touched by her presence. Marion saw, felt and acknowledged me. Now I know that she evoked memories of my mother's touch and care when I was very young. At the time, with Marion, I simply felt accepted. That day I asked her if she would teach me her work and she assured me she would call when there were enough students for a training class. Meanwhile, I continued to get private sessions from her. I also took whatever classes she offered.

On September 3, 1980, our daughter Laurie was killed in an automobile accident. She was nearly nineteen years old. On September 4th, I received a call telling me that Marion was starting her training class and was asked if I still want to be included. Yes.

I don't know how I got through those seconds, minutes, hours, days, weeks - years. But I do know that I felt a great desire to learn Marion's work and that the support and love I felt during those months helped to sustain me through the most unrelentingly painful time in my life. I can't say how I learned the work except to say I absorbed it. Being touched and touching others helped me learn and heal, beyond what words can say. There were no words for the grief I was feeling. Touching, however, began the healing of my broken heart and rendered soul.

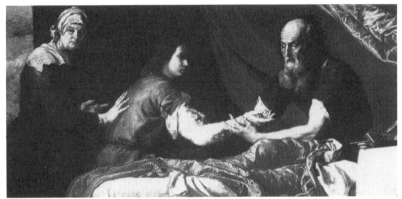

The Blessing of Jacob, Jusepe De Ribera, The Prado, Madrid

The Nature of Touch

The Power of Touch

The greatest sense in our body is our touch sense. It is probably the chief sense in the processes of sleeping and waking; it gives us our knowledge of depth or thickness and form; we feel, we love and hate, are touchy and are touched, through the touch corpuscles of our skin.
Lionel J. Taylor, The Stages of Human Life

As I learned for myself, touch is so basic, so integral to our survival and well-being that very little thought is given to it, even though we use our sense of touch to *experience* life. Technical descriptions alone do not inform us of our experience. For instance, only by exploring the impact air has upon us physically and emotionally, do we begin to understand its essential life-giving, inspirational nature. In order to describe the effect air has upon us as we walk through it and breathe it into our bodies, we use the sense of touch, *i.e.*, proprioception, the internal physical sense of ourselves. When we understand the emotional impact of air upon us we say we are inspired, we feel deeply touched.

It is well documented that touch is the earliest sense developed. Ashley Montagu, in his landmark book, *Touching*, writes:

> Touch is the sense most closely associated with the skin, the most important of all our organ systems next to the brain. The skin in common with the nervous system arises from the outermost of the three embryonic cell layers, the ectoderm. It is the general surface covering of the body and gives rise to the hair, teeth, and the sense organs of smell, taste, hearing, vision and touch...we [might] think of the skin as the external nervous system...the in-turned portion of the general surface of the embryonic body. The nervous system is, then, a buried part of the skin, or alternatively *the skin may be regarded as an exposed portion of the nervous system*. (Montague 2)

Deepak Chopra, a medical doctor from New Delhi, founder of the American Association of Ayurvedic Medicine, and prolific researcher and author, states that:

> In fact, there are neurobiologists who say there is no difference between the immune system and the nervous system - the immune system is a circulating nervous system. It thinks, it has emotions, it has memory, it has the ability to make choices and to anticipate events. (Chopra 18)

While we cannot directly touch either the central nervous system, or the immune system, through touching the skin and meeting the muscle underneath, both are physically influenced through the movement, just like laying your hand on top of a stack of fabric, for instance, would move all the layers underneath.

Touch also educates our vision [through helping us to] discover size, shape, location and distinctiveness. Vision only becomes meaningful on the basis of what [has] been felt....(Montague 250)

Within the womb, the child is deeply affected by being physically and emotionally touched by the mother. Through this contact the fetus develops an individual rhythm and style of responding. Research continues regarding the growth and development of the fetus, and it is widely believed that with the experiences of physical touch and of being touched through sound and light in utero, the fetus begins the development of her/his personality. (Verny 38-39) "Maternal emotions [as well] etch deeply on the fetus and follow the child throughout her/his life". (Verny 25) Children's experience in the womb and during birth has a profound influence on how they will view the world, make choices and live their life.

After birth, it is through the skin that we perceive the world outside of us. Through the skin we define our individual physical boundaries as well as develop our personalities. Touch is as essential after birth as it is inside the womb. We cannot live without it for through touch our physical bodies develop and, psychologically, we learn who we are. How we feel and think about ourselves and how we respond to the world is profoundly influenced by the type and frequency of touch we received as children.

Lack Of Touch

Without touch a baby dies, the human heart aches, and the soul withers.
Phyllis K. Davis, The Power of Touch

Much of our information on touch has come through research done with animals. This research, done primarily with rodents and mammals, has given insight into the essential necessity of touch for humans. For instance, animals who are not licked at birth are most likely to die of a functional failure of the genitourinary system (Montague 15); lack of gentle touch results in fearful, excitable animals; and lack of physical contact causes the pituitary gland to secrete fewer hormones. One of these hormones is prolactin, associated with the initiation and maintenance of nursing. (Montague 21)

Obviously then, lack of touch between mother and child not only affects the child, but affects the mother's ability to nurse the child. Another of the hormones is adrenocirticotropic (ACTH), which initiates the secretion of cortisone by the adrenal gland. This hormone gives relative immunity to stress damage. With only limited amounts of ACTH, the body is prone to cardiovascular and other organic damage under prolonged stress. (Montague 24)

Emotional damage is also inherent with lack of touch. Thomas Verny, M.D., author of *The Secret Life of the Unborn Child*, states that what a mother is thinking and feeling about her unborn child makes an essential difference, for broad and deeply rooted tendencies , such as a sense of security or self-esteem, are being formed in utero. (Verny 29) Continual patterns of clear-cut, intense negative thoughts and emotions can create the kinds of conditioned learning that will negatively affect a child. (Verny 29)

The effect of emotional neglect in utero creates lifelong scars, since the child's mind is shaped by the mother's thoughts and feelings in such a fundamental way. Verny writes:

Studies of schizophrenic and psychotic women testify eloquently to the devastating effects of emotional neglect in utero.... The effects of mental disease make meaningful communication with their children impossible.... At birth [these babies] tend to have far more physical and emotional problems than the babies of mentally healthy women. (Verny 27)

Neglect because of mental illness is at one end of the spectrum. At the other end, there are mothers who themselves feel frightened or lonely and who perhaps do not want a child at all. These pregnancies often leave the fetus bereft of acceptable, let alone loving, communication and comfort. Such an experience is a lonely, helpless existence indeed, one which creates emotions that may haunt the person for the rest of life.

In the extreme, antisocial and /or criminal tendencies develop; more commonly, fetal neglect is often exhibited through an inability to create meaningful and lasting relationships in adulthood. The effects of neglect in utero were determined by Verny through hundreds of studies. He writes that there are three separate communication channels: psychological, behavorial and sympathetic. (Verny 81) The second channel, behavorial communication, is the easiest to observe; for instance, studies have documented that unborn babies kick when they are uncomfortable, frightened, anxious or confused. (Verny 81) The third is sympathetic communication. "The hardest to define, it almost certainly contains elements of the first two, but it is broader and deeper. Love is a good example," he states. (Verny 81-82) Some of his studies were done through ultrasound, showing the fetus's response to maternal thoughts and reactions. (Verny 76) Others were done through case studies that showed bonding had not occurred between the infant and mother; it was not unusual to discover these children were not wanted. In some cases, a tragedy had occurred in the mother's life that took her emotional attention away from the fetus. (Verny 77-79)

In-utero experiences as well as how a child is born - whether it is a painful or easy birth for the child, smooth or violent - largely determines who he/she becomes and how he will view the world around him. (Verny 97) A dramatic study, conducted by Dr. Sarnoff A. Mednick, director of the Psykologisk Institute in Copenhagen, used male subjects who had committed violent crimes. He found the one common denominator among them to be birth history. Fifteen of the sixteen most violent criminals had experienced extraordinarily difficult births. The sixteenth had an epileptic mother. (Verny 105)

On a less dramatic scale, even for those of us who had relatively easy births, too often our exuberance and aliveness is not acceptable in our families. For numerous reasons as infants, we need or want "too much" and make demands through crying or expressing our feelings without restraint. The message to us, occasional or continual, that we are "too much," comes in many forms from our parents and caretakers. Through a harsh tone of voice or a stern look, we are deeply touched and taught that we are wrong. (Wooten 9) What a difficult lesson this is to learn, for we have to be taught we are not acceptable as we are. Some children have even worse experiences: they are physically, sexually and/or emotionally abused. It is possible to read in the newspaper every day examples of abuse.

A startling account in the *Rocky Mountain News*, a major newspaper in the Denver area, told of "Denver's Biggest Crime Family", (Carnahan 20A-24A) it tells of fifteen out of eighteen children who have arrest records. While the crimes on record are robbery and burglary, the real crimes occurred when they were children. "It is a sad litany of physical and sexual abuse, of an absentee father and a mother powerless to stop the ugliness consuming her family", reported Ann Carnahan who interviewed the surviving members of the Bueno family. Della Bueno was raised from infancy by a couple, not relatives, who "weren't very friendly toward her". She married a man of 27 when she was 14 to get out of a this bad situation and after this ominous beginning, gave birth nearly every year of her marriage. The story continues of the children abusing each other through threats, terror and sexual activity with many of them later neglecting or abusing their own children. The legacy endures.

While sensational, this article is an exception only in numbers. It is well documented that abusers of children have themselves been abused in childhood. There seems to be no scale, no way to say exactly that one type of abuse is more or less damaging to the victim.

The Healing Effects of Touch

> Touch must be experienced positively for it to be therapeutic. In that regard, therapeutic touch must be appropriate to the situation and must not impose a greater level of intimacy than the client can handle. It is necessary that therapeutic touch does not communicate a negative message.
> **Willison & Masson, The Role of Touch in Therapy**

Montagu writes of the extraordinary frequency of his coming upon accounts of breakthroughs for schizophrenics that were brought about by body contact. These were patients who had for years been inaccessible through other therapeutic approaches. Paul Roland, a physical therapist at the Veterans Administration Mental Hospital in Ohio, reported success with a catatonic schizophrenic by first sitting with the patient and touching his arm and later, giving him a rubdown.... (Montague 220) Another therapist found that she was able to break through to schizophrenic children by embracing them (Montague 220), while still another therapist discovered that massaging an apparently autistic boy had quicker [therapeutic] effect than any other techniques attempted. (Montague 220)

As healthy newborns, we come into the world moving from the top of our heads to the tip of our toes with every breath we take: the easy, relaxed action of the diaphragm not only moves our breath through us, but provides a movement that reverberates, touching us throughout our entire body. We are open and expressive. (Wooten 62) Conversely, an emotionally distraught child enters the world with breathing patterns already impacted by tension, uncertain and anxious at the beginning of life. (Verny 45-49) For example:

A male client, in his 30s, came to me for bodywork. His face and body looked stoic to me, as if nothing on the face of this earth would impact him. He seemed watchful in such a way that all of his movements, responses, and reactions were affected. The tension in his face belied his age, making him look like an old man, barely able to move, in any way whatsoever, through life. During a Rosen session, the only time I ever saw him relax for even a moment, albeit slight, the words came to him, "I will not breathe !" While he expressed no memories of intrauterine experience, he clearly recalled his moment of birth. He reexperienced how he felt as the people around him attempted, in every way they knew, to start his breathing, and his abject refusal. For thirty-some years his mantra has been, "I will not!" This lifelong stance, while a mystery to his mind, seemed to be fully formed in the cells of his body and exhibited through his posture and attitude. Gentle touch has helped begin the untying of this Gordian knot.

Another male client re-experienced the fear he felt as a child, giving voice to the loneliness and loss he has known all his life. A man in his 50s and successful in his career, Jack said to me, "I've felt nearly debilitating frustration in the search for myself. My mother didn't want to be pregnant and didn't touch me very much after I was born, my father was paralyzed and couldn't touch me. I still don't know who I am." While we may never know what happened in utero or during birth, from his earliest memory to the present, he has suffered from physical tension and emotional frustration. His body, as I worked with him, was particularly narrow around his rib cage from contracted muscles, and as he felt this embodied internal experience of frustration, tears came, then his breathing became easier. He said he had never connected the tightness in his body with his feeling of frustration. As he sensed how his body had "held on" in order to survive in his family of origin, the tension eased along with the feeling of frustration, and he began to breath easier.

Researchers at the newly created Touch Research Institute at the University of Miami School for Medicine have explored, with promising preliminary results, the potential for touch therapy on promoting growth in premature babies. In one recent research program, pre-term infants in incubators were massaged for 15 minutes a day for 10 days. They gained 47 percent more weight than the low-weight babies that were not massaged. These babies were also more responsive to social stimulation and showed better motor development. Similar studies have found beneficial effects with babies born to cocaine-using mothers, HIV-exposed infants and those with depressed mothers. Another program has had good results encouraging communication by autistic children. (Kenen)

Researchers have had exciting results involving boosting levels of serotonin - a neurotransmitter - as well as raising the number of killer cells in men carrying the AIDS virus. Both are vital in the body's immune responses. This is the first time anyone has ever produced growth in the killer cells without drugs. (Kenen)

The Touch Research Institute has also found that elderly people may benefit more from gently massaging babies than from being massaged themselves. (the "massage" referred to here is better described as gentle touch.) Many of the elderly are retired, widowed or isolated and so are "touch-deprived." The researchers found that not only did the babies benefit with improved sleep, better dispositions and lower stress levels, but the volunteer grandparents were also affected positively. Anxiety and depression declined, they drank less coffee, made fewer trips to the doctor, and their social contacts and self-esteem increased. These effects were more pronounced when the volunteers were the ones giving the therapy than when receiving their own daily massage. (O'Sullivan 12)

In March of 1994, Judy Muller of ABC News reported on World News Tonight with Peter Jennings, about the benefits of touch during surgery. She interviewed Dr. Stephen Turner, an ophthalmologist, who has several elderly women as volunteer hand-holders on his staff. In six years they have held nearly 2.000 hands through high-tech eye operations. Margaret Pickford, a hand-holder at the age of eighty-five for Dr. Turner, says she holds hands because, "If you can hold somebody's hand, you can do something for somebody. It's as simple as that." She says her services are rarely refused. Another volunteer says, "I can literally feel the patient letting go of tension and their nervousness and they relax." Dr. Turner states that his patients are less apprehensive. Their blood pressure doesn't shoot up as much and their pulse is not as rapid. And the patient who was interviewed said, "The touching part - her warm hands, smooth hands, [felt wonderful] like she could just hug me and say everything is going to be okay now." What can't be conveyed through the written word is the expression of gratefulness and ease on the patient's face as she related her experience and the look of joy in the hand-holders' eyes. (Muller 4-5)

One more example of the healing power of touch comes from a student of mine, an Occupational Therapist, who works with children with learning problems. She documented her experience:

In my work as an Occupational Therapist with learning problem and physically impaired children, I use some touch and breathing. [These children] are mainly hyperactive, some [are] hypoactive, and most have difficulty concentrating. I have each child, in his/her initial session with me, lie down on a mat and place his/her hands on his/her chest and belly. Often, I place my hands over the child's. I ask the child to close his/her eyes and feel [the movement of] his/her breathing. This slows the child down so he/she can better concentrate. Then we do some postures [which help with] balance, strength, and coordination. While teaching them the postures, I have my hand/s on them and remind them to notice their breath. I have noticed, over the years, that with touch, (both mine and theirs) and by paying attention to their breath, the child becomes more attentive and slowed down, bringing more self-confidence as well as improvement to their strength, balance and coordination. They become more open, spontaneous and creative. (Jacobs)

Touch gentles us, calms us, and give us rest if even for only a moment. Touch can heal us. It brings us back to ourselves, whether we are the one touching or the one being touched.

Somatic Resonance:
The Mandorla Theory

My interest in touch led me to enroll in the practitioner training taught by Marion Rosen. This evolved into a teacher's training and by the end of 1981, I had co-taught my first class, one semester, at John F. Kennedy University. From there, I began teaching workshops in California, then also in Scandinavia. In 1988 a friend and colleague, Sue von Baeyer, Ph.D., Clinical Psychologist, and I taught a course for Rosen Method students entitled "Similarities and Differences between Rosen Method and Psychotherapy". Sue and I had begun our discussion of this topic three years earlier and by 1986 were meeting once a week to further our investigation. We had many questions about the differences and the interface between the two modalities and began our inquiry by defining each separately. For instance, it was clear to us that Rosen Method is not psychotherapy, but is therapeutic: with Rosen Method we do talk with our clients, but rather than face to face as in psychotherapy, the client is lying on a table and the Rosen practitioner is touching her/him; rather than working with "issues" or an agenda, the Rosen practitioner responds with touch, and sometimes with words, to what is happening, in the moment, for the client.

We found that Rosen students were very curious about the relationship between psychotherapy and Rosenwork and also wanted more information about how to create and maintain the therapeutic environment of a Rosen Method session (an environment of acceptance, caring and commitment). With this information, Sue and I developed an outline for the class. We began with Sue teaching child development theory and we integrated information about physical tension, posture and attitude into it. We presented theory about transference and counter-transference, as well as therapeutic boundaries. We discussed the differences in verbal interaction between practitioner and client in psychotherapy and Rosenwork and this became a topic of deep interest for both the students and myself.

I knew, through working with and talking with Rosen students, that many were under the misconception that the verbal interaction between practitioner and client in Rosenwork was based on intuition or getting "psychic hits." For instance, a student once said to me, "Thoughts just come to me when I touch my client. I don't know where they come from, but I'm developing my intuition and becoming a channel." Some students did have psychic abilities and used them while doing what they thought was Rosenwork.

I wanted to dispel this notion many students had, for by thinking they were working with intuition or psychic phenomena, they were misunderstanding the basic theory of Rosen Method. They were not learning, and/or integrating what they had learned about the body, how to make contact with tight muscles and follow the breath.

Most of *my* experience of interacting verbally with clients came from the physical responses I felt in their bodies. *Still*, it was not uncommon to have thoughts come to my mind or feel sensations in my body that seemed connected with the client, but were not related to me in any way I was aware of. I could not find words to explain or define this, either to myself, or our students. I felt stuck and very frustrated and thought about this phenomenon a lot; I questioned my experience and I talked with Sue, but no answers came until after we had already taught our first evening.

I will never forget the morning after our first class. It was a beautiful day and as I sat at my kitchen table gazing out the window at a clear blue sky, I found the answer I had been searching for. Even though I had known, since I was a child, that being touched was important, I felt stunned with certainty, at that moment, of the deep, intrinsic value of "touch." I was overwhelmed with this certainty and a feeling of joy enveloped me. I knew in that moment, when one person touches another, both are deeply effected forever. In this joy and astonishment, the word resonance came to me.

The revelation happened like this: I had paper and pencil in front of me and it occurred to me that if I drew a picture I might see something that I could not formulate otherwise. I drew stick-figures of a client lying on a table, and the practitioner sitting in the chair next to the table, with hands on the client. I drew a large circle around them both.

Then I reflected on my own experience.

I, as the client, am:

- self-absorbed;
- sensation oriented (proprioceptive);
- aware of practitioner's touch;

I, as the practitioner, am:

- consciously aware of touching the other;
- listening in a focused way;
- seeing in a sightly diffused manner;
- feeling occasional prickling of my skin;
- acutely aware of the physical manifestations of movement in client's muscles and breath;

- often noticing my attention being drawn to where my hand touches the client's body.

I then drew a circle around just the table, then a circle around just the practitioner, including the hands which were on the client's body. What I saw was the *overlapping area of the two circles*. The overlap was where the hand was on the body.

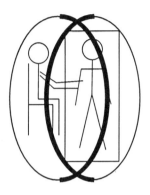

When I saw that, the word *resonance* came to my mind and I knew that was the answer I had been looking for.

At this point I ran to get the dictionary and this is what I found:

RESONANCE: The phenomenon exhibited by any vibratory system responding with large amplitude to a series of *imposed* vibrations of equal or nearly equal frequency.

RESONANT: Sending back or having the quality of sending back or prolonging sound. Resounding, echoing.

RESONATE: (In physics) To manifest sympathetic vibration.

It was then clear to me that the gentle touch of Rosen Method, which simply *meets* the tension in the body, corresponded with the definition of resonance: a series of imposed vibrations of *equal or nearly equal frequency*. With this type of touch and the ensuing resonance, I postulated that several levels of communication take place. On the physical level, touch manifests a sympathetic vibration, which then resounds on emotional and spiritual levels. I concluded that in this state of resonance, two people experience a profound level of communication.

To my amazement and delight, when I told the class of my discovery that night, a student, well educated in religious and symbolic studies, explained that the opening created where the two circles overlapped was called a mandorla, *an opening, or gateway.*

This spoke directly to my own experience: the place where hand meets body creates some sort of opening.

Further research led me to learn that resonance was also known in psychotherapy, spiritual practices and physics. In psychotherapy, the term *affective resonance* is used for the matching that takes place on the emotional level. In spiritual practices, the term *epiphany* means a sudden manifestation or perception of the essential nature or meaning of something. In the physical, somatic realm of touch, I have coined the term *somatic resonance* to define the matching that takes place with gentle, therapeutic (Rosen Method) touch, between the client and practitioner, allowing enhanced inward attention and perception for both.

I continued my research by reading everything I could find on the mandorla. I found it is the almond-shaped segment that appears when two circles overlap and is the Italian word for almond. As Robert Johnson states in his book, *Owning Your Own Shadow,* this symbol signifies nothing less than the overlap of the opposites. (98) I discovered that in early Christian times the mandorla was also known as Vesica Piscis, the vessel of the fish, an early Christian symbol. (Walker 16) It was also known as the yoni, the female creative force and the source of all creative action. (Walker 18) From very ancient times, almonds were female genital symbols and maternity charms. The yonic meaning of this sign was well known in the ancient world and carried such sacred overtones that Christian artists seized upon it to frame the figures of saints, the Virgin, or Christ. Christian mystics redefined the mandorla as the arcs of two circles, left for female matter, right for male spirit. The mandorla is also used to portray a flame, signifying the Spirit or a manifestation of the spiritual or soul principle. (Cooper) And, the mandorla was also sometimes interpreted as a gateway to heaven. (Walker 11)

Johnson suggests that in today's world the mandorla instructs us in how to engage in reconciliation. By paying attention to what we call good and evil, light and dark, we can begin to notice where they touch and overlap. It is through this knowledge and awareness that healing begins. "The Mandorla binds together that which was torn apart and made unwhole-unholy. [Healing the split] is the most profound religious experience we can have in life." (Johnson 102) The third eye is a mandorla and to emphasize this, Johnson quotes from the Scriptures, "If thy eye be single, thy whole body shall be filled with light."

Simply stated in Rosen Method terms, two people come together, one being with, and guiding the other, through touch. It is a quieting experience which allows inner observation and awareness. Two people, with overlapping intentions, connecting through gentle, therapeutic touch, appear to create a profound opening or gateway to inner knowing.

Rosen Method Bodywork

I knew about the opening or gateway through my own experience when I received the initial session with Marion Rosen. I became aware of profound proprioception, which allowed me to have a total inward focus. Her touching me with reverent presence allowed my gentle inner unfolding and her quiet words led the way, not as an inquiry into my mind, but a signal to my body and my unconscious knowing. Her softly spoken "uh-huhs" were like the bread crumbs Hansel and Gretel strew along the path so they could find their way home. (Wooten 69)

I realize now that Marion registered the changes in my body as they began to emerge from unconsciousness to consciousness. She did this by noticing, with her eyes, and feeling, with her hands, the small, and sometimes large, shifts in my breathing pattern and muscular tension. Marion understood that, "The breath is the bridge between the conscious and unconscious" and that through gentle, contactful touch, a person's natural breathing pattern could be freed. Her life experiences and her skill, gained through working with the breath for many years, guided me through her hands and her verbal responses to what she was noticing. There was a *resonance* between us that allowed a deep connection within me and a profound sense of safety. I felt open to my own experience of myself. I remember going away from this initial session with a new awareness of myself and a wonderful feeling of inspiration and well-being. Subsequent sessions engendered the same result, but followed different paths. Each time, I experienced an opening within myself, a gateway through which memories sometimes emerged. Often this would happen a few days after the session. Sometimes, I simply left the session relaxed and increasingly able to notice my responses and reactions during the week. Once in a while I would leave feeling my anger or sadness, but during the week, would sense an inner reconciliation: I reexperienced the parts of myself, through my body, mind, and/or emotions, that had been long forgotten and carefully stored away. Remembering allowed me the choice of either integrating these experiences into my present life, if appropriate, or, letting them go.

During several sessions, I experienced incredible joy and, once in a while, a deep sense of thankfulness and *grace*. In these moments, I could breathe and move with ease, and I felt *fully* alive, as if all the barriers I had created in my being to protect myself no longer were necessary. I could sense *myself* through an inner, physical resonance, and I felt whole and deeply connected to the essential nature of being.

This all seemed mysterious to me until I learned, in my training, the skill needed in order to allow a client to deepen into their own experience. While Rosen Method practitioners are trained in the art of being present with another person, and have the intention of doing so in a fully accepting, respectful, and non-intrusive manner, still, the work is grounded on the knowledge of how the body works regarding muscular tension and individual breathing patterns. During a Rosen session, the practitioner's hands make firm contact with the body, and at times, gently moves different areas to remind the body of the range of movement that is possible when tension is no longer needed. The response that the practitioner looks for is relaxation of the muscle under the hand,

and/or a shift in the movement of breath. For the clie
be experienced as being able to breath easier and/or re
cal discomfort or pain.

Rosen Method looks like massage in that the client lies on a massage table and is touched by another person. However, no oil is used in this work, pillows are sometimes used to increase comfort, the client is partially clothed, always wearing underpants, and if preferred, may leave on whatever clothing s/he wants. The client is then covered with a light blanket for comfort and warmth. The session usually begins with the client lying on his/her stomach and s/he will usually be asked to turn over later in the session, which lasts fifty minutes. Some practitioners stand, others sit next to the table.

When I give a client a Rosen session, I put my hands on top of the cover to start. Then, as the client begins to relax and become more comfortable, I fold the cover down and work directly on the body, usually beginning on the upper back, but taking time to notice and feel where the tension is held. One hand is used for contacting the tension, and the other hand usually rests and "listens."

Some indications of tension are: reduced movement of the solar plexis, the area where the diaphragm is located, or a raised area caused by a contracted muscle. Body temperature, color and texture also tell about internal tension, constricted movement and its effects on circulation. For example, cold hands imply contracted muscles, which constrict blood vessels in the thoracic area. These are also the muscles that allow us to lift and carry, reach out to take or give, to embrace or push away. When we "hold back" here, all of these possibilities are restricted. A tense area may have a drawn, shiny appearance. It may feel "hard as a rock." Sometimes the tension is not obvious at first. Everything may look "just fine" on the outside, but gentle exploration discovers a layer of tension below the surface.

Other ways I notice that the body is not relaxed is through the client's position on the table. For example, the client's chest may not rest comfortably on the table, implying tension in the upper chest as well as across the shoulders in the back. One hip may appear higher than the other, or legs may be held tightly together, giving the appearance of a "pillar", rather than of two legs that move independently of each other. I often tell the client what I'm noticing. I sometimes talk about how a particular area of the body would rest or move if the tension wasn't there.

When I am working with a client, I notice the shape and posture of her body, and it tells me a great deal about her life experiences and how she presents herself in the world. The familiar physical pain or discomfort experienced speaks directly to chronic tension. I watch, feel and listen with rapt attention to the client while at the same time drawing on my own experience, internal awareness and knowledge in order to assist in the unfolding of the client's process.

The questions that are always in my mind are: Who would this person be without their tension? What hurts? What does the shape and posture of this body tell me? What is the potential for movement and expression if this muscle relaxes?" My attitude is one of "not knowing", non-judgment and curiosity. I am there as an observer, witness and facilitator of the client's experience. The result of my intention, attention and knowledge is the creation of a safe place for the client, allowing, over time, for trust to deepen. In this environment, the client begins to listen to him/herself in a new way.

The practitioner will often verbally respond to the changes happening in the body in order to increase awareness for the client. S/he might say, "This muscle under my hand just softened", or "Your shoulder just let go (or tightened). What happened?" The practitioner uses words sparingly to enhance awareness, not to interpret. If the practitioner feels a muscle change, she may simply say, "Yes", in a soft voice. This acknowledges that a change has occurred but without interrupting the inner process. The "Yes" is a suggestion to the client to notice what else is happening, i.e., a thought, an image, an emotion or a familiar or unfamiliar physical sensation. Such noticing allows a person to tap into the unconscious process, much like being in a "waking dream". Sometimes there is an experience of a felt sensation, a memory or deep insight. Often, the client will talk about what she experienced at that moment. The practitioner listens carefully to what the client is saying while watching and feeling the responses in the body to what is being said. At this point, more may be said, either by the practitioner or the client, in order to continue an unfolding of the inner experience. Often it becomes clear to the practitioner, by observing the changes in the body and/or the facial expression, that the client has made the connection on her/his own and nothing more needs to be said.

We often learn to express our emotions with force or effort, causing tension throughout our body. In Rosen work, as our muscles relax and the 'grip' lets go, we have the opportunity to honestly feel the emotion as it is in the moment and to touch the depth of it. Sometimes there are words that express what is deeply felt; sometimes the experience is beyond words. As this process happens, we experience more breathing space, both physically and metaphorically, for the diaphragm no longer needs to hold on so tight.

As clients embody the work, they learn about themselves and they learn to identify what is truthful in themselves. The awareness gained, along with the knowledge, touch and presence of a Rosen Method practitioner, allows a deep relaxation to occur where balance, ease and well-being can manifest. Often there is an accumulation of tiny changes and the client will simply notice, at some point in the work, that s/he is feeling better and that living his/her life doesn't take as much effort as before.

Rosen Method is a process that is gently self-revealing for clients, allowing reflection of their true being, recognition of their integrity and aliveness and the barriers that restrict them. This, in turn, allows awareness and choice. The work provides an environment of self-discovery and profound insight, where "listening" to the inner self and remembering includes, but does not limit itself to, sensations, images and memories. It becomes possible for the client to re-establish a conscious and personal sense of her/his inner process and a deep connection with self-trust and knowing.

Somatic resonance occurs whenever one person *meets* another, through touch. With Rosen Method bodywork, because there is a *conscious* meeting of tensions, the resonance often becomes noticeable. My experience, while touching a client with focused but relaxed attention, is an altered state of consciousness. While in this altered state, I become aware of subtle levels of communication between us. This awareness may come as a thought or sensation of my own which, when communicated to the client, speaks directly to his/her immediate experience. A question may come to my mind or the words of a song may make themselves known, repeating until I speak them out loud. These words, while generally having no impact for me, often have a specific meaning for the client.

I also often match in my own body what the client describes is happening in his or hers. For instance, a client recently spoke of feeling rejected. While I certainly understood the words she spoke, it was when I allowed myself to notice what rejection felt like inside myself that I had some knowledge of what my client was experiencing in her body. The experience literally took my breath away, my shoulders curved forward, and my low back got very tight. I felt my calves contract and toes curl under. I was gripped in the physical experience of rejection. While we were not having the same experience, it was similar enough for my understanding to increase and that allowed my touch to be more specific. At the same time, my awareness shifted with this internal information. I knew more about this person. Going inside myself deepened my connection with her and a sympathetic communication was able to take place on a level that wasn't possible before. I *was touched* and a shift happened between us that allowed the resonance to deepen.

Communication through somatic resonance flows in both directions. As I relax, the environment shifts so that the client can more easily relax as well. Its as if relaxation is contagious, like a yawn. Through relaxation, the resonance seems to deepen, although perhaps what happens is that both my clients and I simply become more "tuned in" and aware of the profound ways in which we are touching each other.

While touching a client I am often aware of my own heightened emotional connection to him/her. The shape of the client's body, the chronic or acute tension I can see and feel under my hands, a story, or even a word or two, can convey the extent to which she/he has had to contract in order to survive; and my experience of all of this seems to come together at the mandorla, where my hand meets his/her body.

The Relationship between Touch, Resonance and Theoretical Physics

I continued my inquiry into the nature of resonance and in so doing, a student, whose husband is a mechanical engineer and does vibrational analysis, sent me the following information:

> Resonant natural frequency is an *inherent* characteristic of an object; it is the frequency at which the objects "likes" to vibrate, regardless of stimulus. This characteristic exists due to the physical nature of the object, its width, length, thickness, and material properties. It is the object's nature.

> Apply a stimulus to the object. If the stimulus carries a frequency component which *matches* the resonant natural frequency of the object, then, the object resonates, or responds at its natural frequency; *the response is typically greater than the stimulus.* If a stimulus is applied to the object, and the stimulus does *not* carry a frequency component matching the natural frequency of the object, *the object does not respond.*

> Modal analysis is the scientific technique used to determine the resonant natural frequency of an object, structure, or system. Usually, the vibrations are too small to be seen but, can be felt.

> In Modal analysis, we use sensing devices to discover the natural frequency of an object, structure, or system. The modal analysis process is:

1) Place vibration sensing devices on the object.

2) Stimulate the object with a known, measurable frequency or set of frequencies.

3) During the stimulation, measure the vibrational response of the object. Select a range of frequencies to search for a response which corresponds to the resonant natural frequency of the object.

If the correct stimulation frequency is used, the object will vibrate at enormous amplitudes, compared to the stimulation. This frequency is "natural" to the object; it is the object's nature.

Another case, known as "forced response", is also possible. If you push hard enough, the object will move, even if it is not the object's nature. This phenomenon is not a resonant condition; it is unnatural to the object. (Marris, Stoneking, Kuo, Bruel & Kerr)

As I read this, it was easy for me to translate this information to the human body and relate this phenomenon to what occurs, through touch, during a Rosen Method session. By meeting the tension in the body through touching, the Rosen practitioner can match the resonant natural frequency of the person being touched, stimulating a vibration that is inherent to the nature of the person.

Interestingly, the article also spoke to what happens when the touch does not meet the natural vibration of the object. Translated to the experience of human beings: if the touch goes beyond "meeting", to pushing, the person will move, but the resonance will not occur. The opening or gateway as described in the Mandorla Theory, cannot happen. I suspect that touch without resonance can decrease human tolerance of such touch to the point of mental, emotional and physical decline, and perhaps, collapse.

The following story relates a stunning example of the effect of enormous amplitudes of vibration to an object:

The Bridge Story

In Washington State the fingers of Puget Sound reach into the tree lined shore. The sound is deep and the currents are dangerous. It is deep enough to accommodate the hulls of huge ships passing through the inlets to moor away from the cold, windy coast. Much of the travel by land is slow. The roads are windy and wander along the coastline of the inlets. In the 1930's, the shipping industry was building a huge shipyard in the city of Bremmerton on the Kitsap peninsula. Tacoma built the Tacoma Narrows Bridge, a suspension bridge, to span a narrow inlet connecting Tacoma to the Kitsap peninsula. The bridge is about one half of a mile long, and is suspended hundreds of feet above the deep water. The winds from the coast carry, with the current, throughout the Puget Sound. They are almost a constant force over the water. The bridge was finally completed by securing a large cable that spanned the crossing. Soon after it's completion, (I think within days), the winds again began their steady passage. This is when people began to notice the bridge humming. The humming went on for a while. The bridge began to rise and fall in height very slightly at first, then the distance it pitched and fell became very exaggerated. This increased into a wavelike pattern. The entire bridge emitted waves that rippled from the Tacoma side to the other. The bridge also rocked in waves back and forth on a horizontal axis. The stress from this began breaking the bolts in the steel and the Tacoma Narrows Bridge began to fall to pieces into the water. It took several days to completely fall apart. If you ever travel across the bridge, there is a small building on the Tacoma side that houses photos and accounts of the whole event. The phenomenon called "flutter" was identified through the study of this collapse. My husband worked at the

Bremmerton Shipyard and did vibrational analysis on the naval ships there. Vibration analysis is a carry-over of flutter analysis. (Shurtliff)

I was reminded after reading The Bridge Story, of a chapter I had read in *The Aquarian Conspiracy*, on consciousness and physics that, while not referring to touch, did acknowledge what happens with the kind of touch I had learned in my Rosen Method training. It also spoke to the subject of resonance and vibration. Ilya Prigigone, a Belgian physical chemist, stated:

> Brainwaves reflect fluctuations of energy. Groups of neurons are experiencing enough electrical activity to show up on the EEG graph. In normal consciousness, small and rapid brainwaves (beta rhythm) dominate the EEG pattern in most people. We are more attentive to the external world than to inner experience in the beta state. Meditation, reverie, relaxation, and other assorted psychotechnologies tend to increase the slower, larger brainwaves known as alpha and theta. *Inward attention*, in other words, generated a larger fluctuation in the brain. In altered states of consciousness, *fluctuations may reach a critical level*, large enough to provoke the shift into a higher level of organization.

> *Memories, including deeply entrenched patterns of behavior and thought, are dissipative structures.* (Italics mine). They are patterns or forms stored in the brain. [Through the study of psychoneuro-immunology it is now known they are stored in the body.] Remember that small fluctuations in a dissipative structure are suppressed by the existing form; they have no lasting effect. But *larger fluctuations of energy cannot be contained in the old structure. They set off ripples throughout the system, creating sudden new connections.* Thus, old patterns are likeliest to change when maximally perturbed or shaken—activated in states of consciousness in which there is significant energy flow. (Ferguson 168-169)

Since Rosen Method allows deep relaxation to occur, I became even more curious about the relationship touch had to altered states of consciousness and Prigigone's statement helped me to understand the *how and why* of memory recall. His words described my own experience in receiving Rosen Method.

Somatically, as I was receiving Rosen Method, I experienced a physical sensation of "settling in" as well as a focused inner attention. As my conscious mind became quiet and I was free of thinking or trying to *figure out* what was happening, and simply became aware of Marion's hand on me, my mind would become quieter still, and I felt as if only the touching existed. In that altered state I was *listening*; it was as if my cells were listening, sensing the touch and rising up to meet her hand. There was no distinction between us at that moment, and then, I would sense a deep fullness within myself. I felt as if an opening occurred and the sea of myself sometimes rippled, sometimes flowed through me. Free of thought, I would feel as if my cells were swimming upstream and would be just on the verge of an awareness, when it would slip away. Sometimes I was overwhelmed with emotion, although no content would appear; other times a word or image would come to me that moved me from the inside out. An "unfolding" is what it felt like. This unfolding had a life force of its own and could not be contained, setting off the ripples of change throughout my system. Each time that happened I felt reconnected to myself in a very profound way: even when there was no specific memory recall, I felt as if, somatically, I remembered something I had always known, but forgotten.

I wanted to understand what was happening. About the same time I discovered Prigigone's statement, I read somewhere that physicists had determined that the basic component of all matter is light. Is that so, I wondered? Could it be that the basis component of each of us is light? This was new and astounding information, and I felt compelled to know more. At this time, I did not know about resonance in relationship to touch and I turned to theoretical physics to see if I could enhance my knowledge of what actually was happening in a Rosen Method session. Certainly, Prigigone as well as Niels Bohr, John Bell and David Bohm, eminent physicists and Nobel Prize winners, were not considering the effects of human touch when they developed their theories on molecular structure, quantum mechanics, non-locality and the implicate order. I became interested in understanding and applying what they discovered to the physiological and psychological dimension: how might physics and touch be interrelated?

I was delighted when I read a story about Niels Bohr who won the 1922 Nobel Prize in Physics for his discovery of the constitution of atoms and molecules, the very beginning of quantum theory. I became curious about this brilliant man: what experiences formed him? What led him, perhaps compelled him, to his discoveries? The following quote, while distracting me from my scientific inquiry of the relationship between touch and physics, caught my attention because it explained something about how he experienced himself:

> Niels Bohr liked to show how a stick used as a probe - a blind man's cane, for example- became an extension of the arm. Feeling seemed to move to the end of the stick, he said. The observation was one he often repeated...because it was charged with emotional meaning for him. (Rhodes 57)

Immediately, upon reading this, I became very curious about Bohr and how he experienced life. Did a connection between sensations, discovery and emotional meaning run throughout his life? I wondered about his life as a child. Was he reared in a loving family? Was touch present or absent? Bohr experienced the connection between his body, an inanimate object and his emotions, *through touch*. While he was described as a person that was profoundly literal-minded, he was also a "child of deep connection" (Rhodes 57) as the quote above suggests. I discovered that interestingly, all of his life, this brilliant man had great difficulty in writing since he laboriously composed on the spot, then drafted and redrafted.

As a child he had trouble learning to write and for many years his mother was his secretary. He dictated his schoolwork to her and later, handed in his master's thesis as well as other scientific papers copied out in his mother's hand. He seems to have suffered greatly from anxiety and was crippled by it for a while. Extreme anxiety seems to have emerged first as "religious doubt and by the time he was eighteen, the doubt had become pervasive and terrifying." (Rhodes 58) I can't help but wonder about the original source of this anxiety. I learned that he was deeply loved by family, friends and colleagues, and yet, it seems something was missing. I don't know how he was touched, emotionally or physically, by those around him, but his anxiety deeply influenced his work throughout his life. I wondered why Richard Rhodes, the author of *The Making of the Atomic Bomb*, prefaced his writing about Bohr with this statement:

> Speech is a clumsiness and writing an impoverishment. Not language but the surface of the body is the child's first map of the world, undifferentiated between subject and object, coextensive with the world it maps until awakening consciousness divides it off. (Rhodes 57)

I could not find an explanation for Rhodes' statement since he did not write about Bohr's infancy. Yet, his dismissal of speech and writing and emphasis on the surface of the body as the primary mode of early learning until one becomes conscious is outstanding to me. What was he alluding to in reference to Bohr, and why did he make this distinction? Perhaps there was something he knew about the care-taking of Bohr who was born in 1885, the first son of a cultured, wealthy and prominent Danish family. Since anxiety is often the result of lack of touch, I can't help but wonder if, in his infancy, loving touch was seldom experienced. Culturally, it's very possible, no matter how loved he was, that he was reared by hired help as well as steeped in a stern environment with little room for emotional expression. A "child of deep connection", reared in an environment where the basic requirements of receiving (and giving) touch are not present and where emotional expression is denied, often experiences deep anxiety.

I'm reminded of a male client, in his early 60's, referred to me by his therapist. His physical appearance belied his profession as a prominent lawyer, as he was small and slightly bent. His quiet manner, bordering on shyness, made an impression on me. I learned he suffered from severe anxiety which had haunted him as far back as he could remember. Years of therapy had helped him to cope, but still, he hoped for some resolution and ease from this debilitating tension. He was interested in physics and spent most of his free time reading about it. He had had few relationships over the course of his lifetime. He spoke of his parents who, he said, loved him very much, hired the best of nannies and later, sent him to the best boarding schools. He has no recollection of being held, holding hands or being touched by his parents other than a peck on the cheek and a handshake as he left for school each fall, beginning at the tender age of eleven. It never occurred to him that his anxiety could have been caused by the lack of loving touch and emotional expression in his family; that in fact, no matter how secure everything looked from the outside, that he had never developed a clear sense of himself and his relationship to the outside world. His body was very tense and the first six sessions we had together brought some ease to him. However, gradually, our work together proved to be too much for him, and the familiar anxiety returned. I realized he simply could not risk relaxing, for he only knew and defined himself through his sensations of anxiety. It was through sensing his anxiety that he knew he existed.

While it is not my understanding that Bohr continued to suffer such extreme anxiety into adulthood as my client, I do believe touch to be such an essential component to well-being that I would be very surprised if loving touch was prevalent in his early life experience.

As I continued my research, I became curious about David Bohm, one of the world's greatest quantum physicists, because he brought together a radical view of physics, a deeply spiritual understanding and a profound humanity. He believed that science is essentially a creative art form that paints dynamic portraits of the natural world, using the human intellect as its canvas and the tools of reason as its palette. (Keepin 11) But what about the influence of *somatic experience* on that palette, I wondered? I extrapolated that a *basic* level of influence on human intellect and reason, missing from Bohm's belief, is what humans experience in their own physical bodies. The primary ways each of us experiences ourselves physically, emotionally or rationally is through proprioception (awareness of inner, felt sensations), by touching ourselves or being touched by another person. And, in fact, *loss of touch with the body results in loss of touch with reality.* (Montague 206) There is no intellect or reason, in fact, there is no "personal identity, substance or structure without the reality of bodily feeling" (Lowen 47)

David Bohm's most significant contribution to science was his ground-breaking theory called *wholeness and the implicate order,* a complex component of quantum physics. This theory postulates that the ultimate nature of physical reality is not a collection of separate objects as it appears, but rather, an undivided whole in which all parts "merge and unite in one totality". (Keepin 11) This undivided whole is not static, but rather in a constant state of flow and change; even mind and matter are united: "In this flow, mind and matter are not separate substances. Rather they are different aspects of one whole and unbroken movement." (Keepin 11) In fact, Bohm believed that each part of physical reality contains information about the whole. Similarly, living and nonliving entities are not separate...." matter does not exist independently from so-called empty space; matter and space are each part of the wholeness." (Keepin 11) In *An Interview with David Bohm,* Bohm is quoted as saying, "What is the point of life if you live in an invented world, if there's no *relationship* either to the world or to the people or to anything? It isn't a relationship if you're related to something which isn't there, or which is just there to make yourself feel comfortable." (Fox) Rosen Method is about relationship, with self and other, developed through touch and resonance.

Continuing with my inquiry, I found that in 1964, the Irish physicist John Stewart Bell introduced Bell's Theorum, the theory of nonlocality, which through experiments showed that *"if distant objects have once been in contact, a change thereafter in one causes an immediate change in the other - no matter how far apart they are, even if they are separated to the opposite ends of the universe. "*(Dossey 84) Physicist Nick Herbert states: ""Bell's theorum *requires* our quantum knowledge to be nonlocal, instantly linked to *everything it has previously touched."* (Italics mine) (Dossey 84)

Bohm said that language imposes strong, subtle pressures to see the world as fragmented and static. He emphasized that thought tends to create fixed structures in the mind. (Keepin 11) My experience is that Rosen Method touch, and the resulting resonance, influences us deeply enough to get through our static and fragmented ways of knowing ourselves to the dynamic core of our own reality (experience). There is no doubt in my mind and bodily experience that when one person touches another, physically or emotionally, the universe changes.

Trance and Touch

Hypnosis and Touch

I was curious throughout my Rosen training as well as in my early-on private practice and teaching about the physical, emotional and attitudinal changes that occurred in my clients. I had experienced it myself time and time again. Often it seemed, my body remembered something which no words or images could convey, and the result was that my posture and the way I moved changed in significant ways: I stood up straighter without effort and, with hips more relaxed, my stride became longer. I became more relaxed altogether and learned to notice the images that unexpectedly came to my mind, both as I was being worked on and after. Sometimes it was several days after a session when a significant memory would emerge from my unconscious. I became very curious about this phenomenon.

In 1988 I was introduced to Eric Greenleaf, Ph.D., a highly respected psychotherapist and teacher of Ericksonian hypnotherapy. We had talked by phone several times about the idea of doing a workshop together, with me doing bodywork while Eric, at the same time, worked with the images that occurred for the client. In preparation for that event, we agreed to experience each others' work. When I met him for the first time I was surprised as I saw him hobble into my office on crutches. He related that he had been struck by an automobile the day before. He was clearly still in shock. He moved slowly and his words, while coherent, were spoken with some effort at concentration. As I worked with him, my hands on his back and shoulders, he relaxed deeply and remembered an event that had changed his life.

Several days later, as I was sitting in a low brown leather chair in his office, he guided me (with words) into a deep relaxation. My experience was similar to how I felt receiving a Rosen session even though his hand was not touching me: My attention was focused inward and I was aware of inner physical sensations. By the time I left his office, my knowledge of what happens in a Rosen session was enhanced. The *altered state of consciousness* I experienced not only quieted my thinking mind, allowing my attention to become focused on inner sensations, but I was not aware of the sounds of traffic passing by or voices in the hallway. I heard only his voice.

It's odd, in retrospect, for I already knew it was not only possible but probable in a Rosen session to enter into an altered state of consciousness. However, the depth of my understanding increased. What I hadn't grasped before was that the altered state of consciousness creates the *pathway* through which our bodies speak to us. The unconscious becomes conscious through inner attention, sensations, images and spontaneous thought. So, as the client experiences the deep relaxation made possible through the touch of Rosen Method, it is possible for unconsciousness to follow this pathway of the altered state to become conscious. This is the primary way in which our bodies speak to us other than through physical discomfort and pain.

As I left Eric's office, I remembered the article by Ilya Prigogine, the Belgian Physical Chemist, (Ferguson 168-169) and I began to wonder if and how there was a connection between what he wrote and my experience. Since touch creates an inward attention, I began thinking about the fluctuations of brainwaves that he referred to. Did he mean that relaxation provokes a shift from beta to alpha and theta, thus allowing memories to emerge? It seemed so to me. I was particularly drawn to his statement that "memories, including deeply entrenched patterns of behavior and thought, are *dissipative structures* ". (Ferguson 168-169) Dissipative means "to scatter, to dispel, to disappear." In Rosen Method we say, "the breath is the bridge between the unconscious and conscious." So, it seems to me that the pathway is: touch to inward noticing, inward noticing to relaxation, relaxation to a shift in brainwaves, a shift in brainwaves to a change in the breathing pattern, and, the change in the breathing pattern to the possibility of bringing from unconsciousness to consciousness our memories, insights and physical shifts in the body. The result is the possibility of moving easier in, and responding differently to, our environment. Physically, this means an easing of physical discomfort. Psychologically, this would include diminishing of the inner critical voice, more ease in making choices, and the ability to respond rather than react. Spiritually, the ease comes through acceptance of one's humanness.

Thinking about all of this, I wanted to learn more about hypnosis. Fortunately, Eric started teaching that fall, and after completing his courses, three other students and I began a consultation group with him that continues to this day. Eric's interest drew him as a young man to the work of Milton H. Erickson, M.D., and he brought his knowledge of Dr. Erickson's work freely and enthusiastically to his teaching and supervision. The context from which he taught matched my Rosen experience and made it possible for me to enhance my learning of psychotherapeutic and hypnotherapy skills and take what was useful into my Rosen practice.

I am sure I would not have had the same response and recognition to the altered state of consciousness had I worked with someone with a different training in hypnosis. Later I discovered there are many different forms and schools of thought about hypnosis, with each school often viewing people in an entirely different light and leading to different observations and recommendations. I was grateful that my first experience with hypnosis was with Eric.

Milton H. Erickson, M.D.

Ronald A. Havens, editor of *The Wisdom of Milton Erickson* writes:

> Erickson redefined the traditional understanding of the conscious and unconscious minds. He argued that the rigid attitudes and restricted awareness of the conscious mind typically is responsible for most human problems and described the unconscious mind as much more intelligent, aware, capable and useful than the conscious mind. He argued that effective functioning requires an open pattern of communication and cooperation between these two separate entities. As a result, his therapeutic goal was to create a climate within which each individual could more comfortably utilize unconscious resources and understandings. (first preface)

And Dr. Erickson did so in his unique style. He challenged earlier theories and assumptions of human behavior and influenced a shift in the understanding of hypnosis.

> He took the time and effort simply to observe what people actually do and what variables actually influence their behavior. He noticed every detail and applied his observations in his practice of hypnotherapy. He devoted his life to careful observation of himself and others and, as a result, he became more familiar with the nature of people than perhaps anyone else before or since. As a consequence, he learned how to enable others to utilize potentials they did not know they had and he helped them resolve personal and interpersonal problems that no other professional had been able to touch. (Havens vi)

While Erickson did not keep his hand on his patients (Erickson, B. A.) as is done in Rosen Method, he was visually aware of ideomotor signaling, *i.e.*, the way the unconscious speaks through the body with nods or movements of hands, arms or legs. In his teaching, he would often relate that he noticed an immobility of the face or a certain rigidity, [or lack of tonicity], and he carefully tracked the breathing pattern of the subject.

He knew that as eyelids began to blink in a certain way the subject was narrowing down his attention, developing an inner focus. (Erickson, Rossi, Ryan 188) 'Subjects [he said] become absorbed in sensing their own psychosomatic phenomena as a personal experience in which they are active. Thus the situation is transformed from one of passive responsiveness for the patient to one of active interest, discovery, integration, and participation in these changes produced by hypnosis. (Havens 101).

Further, he taught his students:

'What is important is your willingness to observe all of these individual patterns of breathing, of holding the face, of holding the head, of holding the hand, and all of the body postural responses that are ordinarily made....' (Erickson, Rossi, Ryan 188)

Thus, he taught his students that the body holds experiences within and speaks to the observer through unconscious physical expressions.

State Dependent Memory

Erickson's concepts of the "neuro-psycho-physiological' basis of therapeutic hypnosis (Erickson, Rossi, Ryan 203) seems to have been first discovered by James Braid (1795-1860), a Scottish physician, who defined hypnotism as a process modern researchers would term "state-dependent memory and learning". State dependent memory and learning theory says that what is learned and remembered is dependent on one's psychophysiological state at the time of the experience. (Erickson, Rossi, Ryan 206) For example: if the client's experience is one of shame, then the memory recall occurs when the client reexperiences the state of shame as felt in his/her physical and emotional being during the time the memory was repressed.

In 1986, Ernest Rossi, Ph.D., an early student of Erickson's, and editor of many volumes of Ericksonian theory and teaching, as well as innovative researcher and author, states:

Since memory is dependent upon and limited to the state in which it was acquired, we say it is 'state-bound information'. (Rossi 38)

Mind and body are both aspects of one information system. Life is an information system. Biology is a process of information transduction. *Mind* and *body* are two facets or two ways of conceptualizing this *single information system*. All methods of mind-body healing and therapeutic hypnosis operate by accessing and reframing the state-dependent memory and learning systems that encode symptoms and problems... This learning and behavior is mediated by the limbic-hypothalamic system. (Rossi 54-55)

Touch coalesces, through resonance, this single information system, allowing the state-bound information to become conscious through relaxation followed by physical ease and memory recall.

Erickson stated:

The induction and maintenance of a trance serve to provide a *special psychological state in which the patient can reassociate and reorganize his inner psychological complexities* and utilize his own capacities in a manner in accord with his own experiential life... Therapy results from an *inner resynthesis* of the patient's behavior achieved by the patient himself.... It *is this experience of reassociating and reorganizing his own experiential life that eventuates in a cure....* (Rossi 67)

In his book, *The 20 Minute Break: Using the New Science of Ultradian Rhythms*, Ernest Rossi states:

Touch may be the most powerful sociobiological signal of all. When we are touched gently and rhythmically, our brains release the feel-good messenger molecules called beta-endorphins and we slip into the psychologically receptive state of the Ultradian Healing Response. We open up to increased intimacy. No wonder that the people we let touch us - massage and physical therapists, barbers and hairdressers, nurses and physicians - are often the recipients of our deepest personal confidences. (Rossi, Nimmons 174-175)

The Creation of Adam, Michelangelo, Sistine Chapel, Vatican

Touch & Creative Expression

As I began teaching I became very interested in including creative activities such as writing or working with clay to enhance the learning experience of my students. My personal experience with creative activity was that I experienced the ultradian rhythm then, just as I did if I were touching a client or being touched myself. Since this altered state of consciousness allowed unconscious process to evolve I knew that by combining touch and creative activity, my student's learning would be deepened.

Students learn Rosen Method experientially by doing hands-on work with each other, watching demonstrations and learning theory. Every day there is a time for group "process sharing" where students have the opportunity to say what they are noticing about their own experiences and emotions. The Intensives are a time of personal insight and integration for students. They learn Rosen Method by learning about themselves; they learn how to be with others by experiencing what holds them back from the intimacy that is a part of touching another person.

Students are touching or being touched by a classmate for a minimum of two-three hours every day and this evokes introspection and proprioception. The Intensives provide a rich and fruitful time for each student, whether they are taking the training for personal growth or professional training. Rosen Method touch "touches" the unconscious and each student has his/her own rhythm of insight and awareness. Working with hands in creative ways not only is a change of pace from the intensity of the classroom, but enhances each person's process of integration.

I wanted to find creative modalities that would enhance each person's personal process, was compatible with Rosen Method, and fit within the time frame. Since I find working with clay quieting to my mind and inspirational to my own creative process, I had local micaceous clay available for students to play with at our first Ghost Ranch Intensive. On the last day of class, each student brought in what s/he had made with the clay and expressed what it meant to them. What I had suspected would happen, did: each student created something with her/his hands that spoke to and brought together her/his individual internal process during the Rosen Intensive.

As they described their creative symbols, expressions of delight, puzzlement and questioning, as well as, wonder, joy, and awe emerged. Some formed fetishes from the clay, others made small bowls, a few made plaques, with words or symbols that were significant to them, written in the clay. They loved working with the clay and wanted more.

I met Felipe Ortega, a Jicarilla-Apache potter and shaman, at the end of that Intensive. He was at Ghost Ranch teaching a pottery class so we were all able to see his work. I asked him if he would teach pot making at the next Intensive. He was delighted to accept and offered to provide a sweat lodge for my students as well. The students' excitement about working with clay and the results, was an acknowledgment to me that involving a creative process in my teaching was significant.

I scheduled two long intensives in 1992 & 1993 which allowed time for Felipe Ortega to join us after class sessions to teach pot making. An entire course was taught on the coil method of pot making, including not only forming the pot, scraping, drying, polishing with a stone, and firing in a pit, but the reverence, spirit and gift of working with Mother Earth. When the pots were completed, Felipe "read" each one, giving the student potter insight into the message of her/his pot. In addition, he also continued to lead sweat lodges for the students. These were, and still are, deeply meaningful experiences, moving each student forward in her/his personal process.

At a later intensive, we made masks, and "danced" them on the final day of class. Students paired up, one shaping the wet, plastered gauze to her/his partners face. On this plaster mask of their own faces, each student applied paint, and some added objects from nature, while others added personal symbols of self-expression with glitter, beads, or objects brought from home.

This too, just as the clay, proved to be a great inroad to personal insight and growth. Before dancing the masks, students gathered in groups of four and with the help of the others in their group, were led in a process of discovery of how they experienced themselves with the mask on and how their bodies felt like moving. The entire class was joyous and amazed at the inner selves that emerged with this process.

Writing is another creative form included in the Intensives. Amazement and delight emerged with this process as students discovered themselves through timed writing, fairytales and fables. Each of these processes added immensely to each students' growth and personal understanding.

Students sometimes continued with creative expression when they returned home, and I found those whose work was in the arts were greatly influenced. One student, a university instructor in the Arts department, created two quilts which were born from her experience at the Intensive. She wrote this artist's statement for an exhibit of her quilts:

Contemporary art rests so much on the top of one's head, a very small space to put so much structure. The quilts are representations of the body, as a container feeling the contents of itself, a visual interpretation of an experiential concept. As an artist using my vocabulary of painting style, medium or content and applying that language to the sensations of bodywork, the results can border on the ridiculous. My mind's attempts at interpreting and rendering these experiences feels trapped in its own limitations. The very attachment of words for description, or images which represent this, is the attachment of a language. The body's realm is a place which has no language, only feeling, nuance, and emotion, and until recently, it is a world I'd chosen to ignore in my adult years. I was hiding in my body all this time, unwilling to attach myself to the heady world. Even this description make this whole process sound like a philosophical discussion, which it is not. Being bored and exhausted with the limitations of the contents of my head, I began looking elsewhere for something interesting. I felt trapped in my head and wanted a new way to interpret myself, my past, present and future. Eventually, I stumbled upon a way to disengage the intellect from my life - whew, what a relief, so much room to relax! Even the effort I've made to write about or represent bodywork has been unsettling and irritating. The academic structure I learned at the university had entrapped me within the very structure that I'd been taught. Over time, the intellectual structure diminished and narrowed the definitions of myself as an artist and my life. The corridors of my mind began rewinding into itself like a continually repeating "muzak" tape.

This new work is indeed in the old package of style and rendering that I've learned from training. I seek to convey a new sense of remembering space, the space and lack of definition within me and the discovery of memories, which include my body. Most individuals have sensed this in their bodies, in a realm when they begin the descent into slumber. (Shurtliff)

The experience of touch and of being touched, both physically and emotionally, is illuminated and amplified by working with clay, making masks, and through timed writing. Being touched, as in Rosen Method, taps into the unconscious, allowing a connection within each person to her/his own creative expression. These modalities of creative expression are self-revealing, as are the images that emerge in hypnosis or through the touch of Rosen work.

Conclusion

My inquiry into the relationship between touch and science, hypnosis, hypnotherapy, and creative expression has not only increased my knowledge of the profound connection between these disciplines, but has inspired me to want to know even more.

I have felt inevitably drawn to explore the connection of touch, not only with consciousness, as Prigigone theorized, but with spirit as well. Reading about David Bohm's inquiry into questions concerning truth, reality, meaning, language and thought which led him to spend much of his later life in dialogue with the spiritual teacher, J. Krishnamurti. (Keepin 10) spurred my interest. Bohm eventually came to believe that the single most important feature of reality is "unbroken wholeness in flowing movement". (Keepin 15)

In my own inquiry I found a significant connection between the body and spirituality when I discovered a book several years ago entitled, *The Mind of the Cells*, written by Satprem. He dedicated his life to writing about the work of the spiritual teacher and visionary, Sri Aurobindo, and his successor, known as "Mother". Satprem recorded, in the course of countless personal conversations with Mother, the log of her exploration in the cellular consciousness of the body; twenty-three years of experiences, which parallel some of the most recent theories of modern physics.

Mother stated that "Salvation is physical"; [one] has to reach the point of the atomic and cellular level. Instead of soaring to nirvanic or celestial heights; one has to break through the [physical] barrier.... (Satprem 59-60) She said. "The body is the bridge. The body, that is, the cells", (Satprem 9) and continues to say, "It seems that one can truly understand [oneself] only when one understands *with* the body". (Satprem 10) In 1970, when Mother was ninety-two years old, she said:

> Now the body has the experience [of consciousness], and it is *much more real*. There is a certain intellectual attitude which puts a kind of veil or...I don't know, something.... unreal over our perception of things: it's as if we were seeing *through* a certain veil or a certain atmosphere, whereas the body feels directly, it *becomes*. It feels in itself. Instead of the experience being scaled down to the measure of the individual, the individual widens to the measure of the experience. (Satprem 158)

Touch is a biological necessity; touch, given in a respectful and contactful manner, relaxes us, leading to insight and expanded consciousness; touch brings us into contact with ourselves and allows an inner journey beyond the known toward a discovery of our essential nature.

My years of working with hundreds of people as a Rosen Method practitioner and teacher have taught me much about the significance and profound nature of touch. I also found that creative expression is enhanced by touch and that through touch and hypnosis, images, along with self-understanding emerge. In addition, the ideas and theories that were brought forth through my inquiry into the relationship between touch and physics highlight and accent the importance of touch as a vehicle of deep understanding.

My unceasing curiosity about touch has led me to this inquiry and book and is, without a doubt, only the beginning. My hope is that what I have written will encourage others who might continue this inquiry.

Bibliography

Carnahan, Ann. "*Denver's Biggest Crime Family*", Rocky Mountain News. August 28, 1994.

Chopra, Deepak. *Timeless Mind, Ageless Body*. <u>Noetic Sciences Review</u> #28. Winter. 1993.

Cooper, J.C.. *An Illustrated Encyclopaedia of Traditional Symbols*. Thames & Hudson, Ltd.. London: 1978.

Davis, Phyllis, K. *The Power of Touch*. Hay House, Inc. Carson, CA: 1991.

Dossey, Larry, M.D. *Healing Words: The Power of Prayer and the Practice of Medicine*. HarperSanFrancisco. New York: 1993.

Erickson, B.A.. Personal conversation. October, 1994.

Erickson, Milton H.. Edited by Rossi, Ernest L. & Ryan, Margaret O.. *Mind-Body Communication in Hypnosis, The Seminars, Workshops, and Lectures of Milton H. Erickson, Vol III*. Irvington Publishers, Inc.. New York: 1986.

Ferguson, Marilyn. *The Aquarian Conspiracy : Personal & Social Transformation in the* 1980's. J. P. Tarcher, Inc.. Los Angeles: 1980.

Fox, Noel, producer & director. *An Interview with David Bohm.* Videocassette. Mystic Fire Video. 1994.

Havens, Ronald A.. *The Wisdom of Milton* H. *Erickson: Hypnosis & Hypnotherapy, Volume One.* Paragon House Publishers. New York:1985.

Jacobs, Ellen. Personal letter. September, 1994.

Johnson, Robert. *Owning Your Own Shadow.* HarperSanFrancisco: 1991.

Keepin, William. " *David Bohm: A Life of Dialogue Between Science and Spirit".* Noetic Sciences Review. Summer; 1994.

Kenen, Joanne. *"Science's Healing Hand: The Benefits of Massage".* The San Francisco Chronicle. February 19, 1993.

Lowen, Alexander, M.D..*The Betrayal of the Body.* McMillan Publishing Co: New York:1967.

Mahler, Margaret S., Pine, Fred, Bergman, Annie. *The Psychological Birth of the Human Infant.* BasicBooks, HarperCollins Publishers. New York: 1975.

Marris & Stoneking. *Advanced Dynamics.* Krieger Publishing Company: 1967.

Kuo, Benjamin C. *Automatic Control System.* Prentice-Hall, Inc:1975.

Bruel & Kerr. *Shock and Vibration Measurement.*

Montagu, Ashley. *Touching.* Harper & Row. New York: 1971.

Muller, Judy. ABC News: World News Tonight with Peter Jennings. EST Edition, Transcript #4053. Air Date: March 16, 1994.

O'Sullivan, William. *"The Gift of Touch."* Common Boundary. May/June; 1994.

Ragghianti, Carlo Ludovico. Editoral Director. *Vatican Museums Rome.* Newsweek, Inc. & Arnaldo Mondadori Editore. Milan; 1968.

Rhodes, Richard. *The Making of the Atomic Bomb.* Simon &Schuster, Inc. New York: 1986.

Rossi, Ernest L.. *The Psychobiology of Mind-Body Healing: New Concepts of Therapeutic Hypnosis*. W. W. Norton & Company. New York: 1986.

Rossi, Ernest, Ph.D with Nimmons, David. *The 20-Minute Break*. Jeremy P. Tarcher, Inc. Los Angeles: 1991.

Satprem. *The Mind of the Cells* . Institute for Evolutionary Research. Ltd., New York: 1982.

Shurtliff, Jen. *The Bridge Story*; personal account: 1994

Venturi, Lionello. Skira, Albert, Collection Planner & Director. *Italian Painting The Renaissance, Volume 2*. Rome: 1951.

Verny, Thomas, M.D., & Kelly, John. *The Secret Life of the Unborn Child*. Dell Publishing. New York: 1988.

Walker, Barbara G.. *The Woman's Dictionary of Symbols & Sacred Objects*. HarperSanFrancisco. California: 1988.

Willison, B.J., and Masson, R. L.. *"The Role of Touch in Therapy: An Adjunct to Communication."* Journal of Counseling and Development #64. 1986.

Wooten, Sandra. *"Rosen Method "*. MASSAGE Magazine #44, July/August; 1993.

About the Author...

Sandra Wooten, M.A., C.M.T., C.H.T., began her studies with Marion Rosen in 1978. She incorporated the Rosen Institute in 1983 and was the founding president of the Board of Directors. In 1986 she began teaching in Santa Fe, New Mexico, and in 1990 founded the **Rosen Method Center Southwest.** She has a private practice in Rosen Method bodywork and Clinical Hypnotherapy in Berkeley, California.

Since 1984 Sandra has taught Rosen Method bodywork and movement in the United States, Europe, Scandinavia, and Russia. Currently, as director of the Rosen Method Center Southwest, Sandra regularly teaches workshops in Rosen Method bodywork for individual personal growth, professional certification, and continuing education. Sandra is also on the faculty of the Milton H. Erickson Institute of the Bay Area, Berkeley, and lectures at conferences and academic symposiums.

Sandra can be reached through the Rosen Method Center Southwest, P.O. Box 344, Santa Fe, New Mexico 87504, (505) 982-7149, or through her Orinda, California, office, (510) 258-0208. Her e-mail address is sw.touch@ix.netcom.com.